Too Many Freckles!

Written by Sally Gomez

Illustrated by Hazel Mitchell

ZOË LIFE
PUBLISHING
WORDS TO LIVE BY

© 2008 Sally Gomez

Published by:
Zoe Life Publishing
P.O. Box 871066
Canton, MI 48187 USA
www.zoelifepub.com

Author: Sally Gomez
Illustrator: Hazel Mitchell
Editor: Jessica Colvin

First U.S. Edition 2008 Softcover, Perfect Bound

Publisher's Cataloging-In-Publication Data

Gomez, Sally
  Too Many Freckles!

Summary: A little boy endlessly teased about his freckles asks God for a miracle. God helps him in a roundabout way and the children learn about kindness, inner beauty, and God's love.

10 Digit ISBN 1-9343633-2-4 Softcover, Perfect Bound
13 Digit ISBN 978-19343633-2-4 Softcover, Perfect Bound

Library of Congress Control Number: 2008931650

For current information about releases by Sally Gomez or other releases from Zoe Life Publishing, visit our web site: http://www.zoelifepub.com

Printed in the United States of America

v5 06 24 08

Dedication and Acknowledgments

I would like to dedicate this book to my grandchildren, great grandchildren and all children everywhere. I pray that as you read this book your lives will be changed.

For the God-given gift to write this book I give all the credit to my Lord and Savior Jesus Christ. To Him be the Glory!

To my wonderful husband Benny, whom I love and cherish, thank you so much for your love and support.

To my dear friend Sheryl, your prayers and encouragement have meant so much.

To all my family, friends and my church, you have been so enthusiastic and supportive.

To all the staff at Zoe Life Publishing, you have been there for me in so many ways. God bless you.

Too Many Freckles!

Written by Sally Gomez

Illustrated by Hazel Mitchell

Table of Contents

Foreword

I have known Sally Gomez since 2004 and have witnessed her storytelling first-hand. To suggest that Sally is a natural storyteller with a childlike wit, and a skill as sharp as a two-edged sword would be an understatement. She transforms the common into the fantastic, the familiar into the new, and what makes children yawn into what makes them laugh. Her audience, anticipating, sitting on curled toes and knees, leaning forward, is never disappointed. The stories seem to come alive. They are magically changed in mid-air from language to life. Surprises are always expected and always appear, but the real wonder is what she teaches. The love that she imparts through her carefully built stories may seem to be hidden to the very young, but we are all fooled. Their storytime joy is just masking what love they absorb, and this is truly appreciated by their parents. Sally is a great gift to us indeed.

—James R Wylie, Children's Pastor
Crosspointe Church
Brooklyn, MI

I have known Sally Gomez for over six years and if there is one thing I can say it's that she has the precious heart of a child. She loves children and she is everyone's grandma. Over the last five years I have seen her grow in her relationship with God and her desire to help children grow in Him. She teaches Sunday school regularly and the kids love her. I am thankful she has such a heart.

—Pastor Daniel Schultz
Crosspointe Church
Brooklyn, MI

Connie was a cute little redhead girl and she'd been in his class ever since preschool. She was always nicer to him than anyone else in the class, no matter how the other kids treated him. She even had freckles too, but only a few. Even though Connie always had a kind word to say, day after day, the other kids would say mean things about Johnny's freckles. Poor Johnny!

One particular day, all day long (or so it seemed to Johnny) wherever he went, some kid was spouting out rude words about his freckles. In gym class, one boy said, "Johnny you can't run fast. Kids with freckles can't run fast. Besides, your freckles are probably too heavy!" Other boys in the gym class laughed along. "Ha! Ha! Ha!" they taunted as they pointed at Johnny.

When it came time for lunch, one girl said, "Be careful not to get too much ketchup on your face, or you will look like one big freckle." Johnny could hear the rest of the girls giggling along behind his back.

Connie walked over and said, "These boys and girls aren't being very nice. Connie smiled and leaned very close to Johnny's face, saying, "Besides, I kind of like your freckles. One thing I know for sure," Connie continued, "is the Lord made us, and we are special to Him. Maybe we should pray for all these kids who are always hurting your feelings—that they learn how to treat others the way they would want to be treated."

"Wouldn't do any good," said Johnny. "I'm just a kid. Why would the Lord help out with this problem? Do you actually think He cares about my feelings?"

"Why sure!" Connie said with a smile. "Jesus cares about everything that concerns us."

Johnny said, "I'm not so sure about that. I have heard that Jesus loves me, but I'm not so sure—my feelings—oh, I just don't know!"

Finally, the school day ended. As Johnny walked out of the school building, the same old gang of boys was waiting for him. When he saw them, he quickly looked around for an adult, but didn't see one. *Uh oh, I'm really in for it*, he thought to himself. You see, this group of boys always acted sugar sweet when a grownup was around, but if they were alone with Johnny, every ounce of sweetness went away. *Hopefully*, Johnny thought to himself, *they won't be so mean since Connie is standing just over there.*

Unfortunately, Connie's presence did not matter. The boys were as rude as ever! But this time, Connie heard the mean boys saying things like, "Freckle Face! Freckle Face! Freckles are not cool! We don't want a freckle faced boy coming to our school! You're contagious!" This made Connie so mad that she ran into the school to find Mrs. Williams.

The boys were pointing at Johnny and taunting him so much that big tears began to form in his eyes. One tear trickled onto his cheek, and Johnny ran as fast as his little feet could carry him away from the school.

By the time Connie and Mrs. Williams got outside to talk to the boys, everyone, including Johnny, was gone. "Well Connie, I guess I'll have to wait until tomorrow to talk to them," said Mrs. Williams.

Johnny ran and ran, faster and faster, sobbing and crying so hard he could hardly breathe. He ran right into Mr. Green's apple orchard, stopping under a very large apple tree. Johnny sat there sobbing as big tears ran down his face. He couldn't brush off the name-calling anymore. As he sat under that tree, Johnny thought back to last fall when they first started calling him names. He realized, *It's been a whole year! I've tried absolutely everything I can think of to get rid of the teasing.*

Once, Johnny decided to use some of his mother's make-up to try and cover his freckles. That was a huge mistake. When he arrived at school that day, the kids really made fun of him. Eddie said he looked like a girl, but he still called him Freckle Head.

Another time, he decided to wear his ski mask to cover up his freckles. Boy, he looked silly wearing *that hat* on a warm October day. Not only that, it just made him hot and itchy.

As he sat under the apple tree thinking, Johnny suddenly remembered what Connie had said about Jesus caring. Johnny began to pray, "Oh, Lord Jesus, if Connie is right and You care about my feelings, then please take my freckles away."

Chapter 2
The Freckles Gang

"Hey, Man," cried Frankie Freckle, "I'm getting all wet!"

"Ugh! Is it raining?" asked Rosey Freckle.

"I don't know," said Annie Freckle, "but I'm getting all wet."

"No, no," said Samuel Freckle. "They're tears. Johnny is crying."

"Calm down, all you freckles!" shouted Pete Freckle. "I just heard from the Lord. The Lord said that He wants us to help answer Johnny's prayer."

"Hmm," said Harry Freckle. "How are we gonna do that?"

"We need a plan and quick!" replied Gigi Freckle.

"I've got it!" said Naomi Freckle. "Remember when Johnny got sunburned on his face last summer and Freddie Freckle the fireman helped us all escape up to Scalp Mountain so we could cool off? Maybe we could do that again!"

Just then, Freddie, the fireman freckle, arrived on the scene. "What's going on?" he asked.

Pete Freckle explained how Johnny had prayed for the Lord to make his freckles go away and how the Lord told Pete that the Freckles gang was to help Johnny.

10

"All right," said Freddie. "Let's get moving." By this time, a huge crowd had gathered to see what was happening. "First," Freddie continued, "all you big, strong football player freckles climb up to Johnny's hair and hold up some hairs for the freckles to climb up. We'll hurry up and off Johnny's face. We will need to climb up as quickly as we can to the highest apples on this tree he's sitting under. We will become the freckles on those apples!" he said. "We have to hurry and get off of Johnny's face before he stops crying."

"The Lord said He is sending some angel freckles to help us get up to the apples quickly," Pete said with excitement.

"Oh good," Freddie replied.

Down came the angel freckles from above. They swooped up each freckle, moving as fast as they could, hurrying to get them off Johnny's face. Then, just as Johnny stopped crying, the very last freckle hopped off of the angel's back onto a tree branch.

"Guess I had better go home," Johnny muttered to himself.

Chapter 3
No More Freckles

When Johnny returned home, his mother asked him where he had been. "Supper is almost ready," she said. Johnny hurried into the bathroom to wash up. As he washed his hands, he looked into the mirror, and much to his surprise, his freckles were gone!

"Mom, Mom!" cried Johnny as he ran into the kitchen. "My freckles are gone!"

"Well, glory be!" she exclaimed.

"Grandma Rose, look! Look, my freckles are gone!" said Johnny. He was so excited, he almost knocked her over when he ran up to her.

"Land's sake! Your freckles are gone!" Grandma exclaimed.

Johnny didn't wait around to hear any more remarks. He quickly ran into the living room to tell Dad and Grandpa Joe. "Dad! Grandpa! My freckles are gone!" he shouted.

"My goodness," exclaimed Grandpa. "How did that happen?"

"Yes, tell us!" said Dad. "How did this miracle happen?"

Johnny started telling his grandpa and dad how the kids at school were making fun of his freckles and calling him names. And how today, when he got out of school, the same three boys who were always calling him names were waiting for him and had really started in on him. He told them that he was so hurt that he started crying and ran away. "My eyes were so blurry from crying that I didn't even notice running into Mr. Green's apple orchard," he said.

12

He told them how he had sat under a big apple tree and cried and cried. He said it was then that he remembered what Connie Sims had told him. "She said that Jesus cares about everything that concerns us, even our hurt feelings. So, I prayed and asked Jesus to take away my freckles, and He did!"

Grandpa said, "Connie is right. Jesus does care about us, and He really did answer your prayer, Johnny. He gave you a miracle."

Johnny heard his mother's voice. "Supper is ready!" she called.

Betsy, Johnny's little sister, came down from her room when she heard their mother call. After everyone was seated, Dad prayed a blessing.

"Lord, we thank You for this food we are about to eat. Bless it and use it to give us strong healthy bodies. And we thank You, Lord, for Johnny's miracle. Amen."

13

"What's a miracle, Dad?" four-year-old Betsy asked.

"A miracle is when Jesus does something supernatural for us, like when He heals us when we are sick," said Dad.

"But what is supernatural?"

"Betsy, supernatural is something only God can do, that we cannot do for ourselves. He does something supernatural because He loves us so much. He really does care about our feelings," Dad answered, smiling at Johnny and touching his face where the freckles used to be.

After supper, everyone helped clean off the table. It was then that Betsy noticed her brother's face. "Johnny, where are your freckles?" she asked.

"That is Johnny's miracle," answered Dad. "Johnny asked Jesus to take away his freckles, and He did."

"I don't like it!" said Betsy. "I like Johnny better with freckles. That's the way God made him, so isn't that the way he's supposed to be?"

"Hmmm," Dad said. "It's true. That's the way God made him. Tell me Johnny, did you hate your freckles or was it the teasing that you wanted to disappear?"

"Gee, I don't know," Johnny replied.

"And why didn't you feel you could tell us that the kids at school were picking on you?"

"Dad…I…I didn't want to worry you. You've been worried about your job and I just thought…"

But Johnny's mother interrupted before he could say any more. "Oh Johnny, we care about you and love you unconditionally the way Jesus does."

"Group hug!!" Dad announced, pulling Johnny, Betsy and their mother into his arms and squeezing tight. There was so much love that Johnny had a hard time choking away the tears.

The next day at school, Johnny was in for a big surprise.

14

Chapter 4
Johnny's Big Surprise

At the schoolyard the next day, Tommy didn't call Johnny any names. Tommy didn't even recognize him when he came over to the swings! Of course, Johnny really did look different without freckles. To add to his freckle-free face, he was wearing different glasses because he had broken his old pair over the weekend. In addition, he had gotten a new haircut—one which was much shorter than his previous style. All of this together really made the old Johnny look like a brand new Johnny.

Tommy walked up to Johnny and said, "Hi, my name is Tommy. What's your name?"

"I'm Johnny Baxter."

"Aw, you can't fool me! You're not Johnny. He has a freckle face."

Eddie was standing nearby and heard what the two boys were saying. He joined in, saying, "You don't look like Johnny Baxter. He has lots of freckles on his face."

15

"But it's true," said Johnny. "I just don't have freckles anymore."

Along came Bojo. "Hi," he said, looking at Johnny. "My name is Bojo."

"Yeah, I know," said Johnny, who by this time was getting upset. "You know me. I'm Johnny Baxter!"

"Yeah, right! If you are Johnny, where are your freckles?" Bojo asked, squinting, and looking for the missing freckles.

"I prayed and asked Jesus to take them away," Johnny replied.

"You've got to be kidding," said Eddie, furrowing his brow in doubt. "You expect us to believe that?"

While they were talking, Connie came over to meet the "new kid" (so she thought). "Hi, my name is Connie," she said with a wave.

"Oh no. Not you, too!" cried Johnny.

"What do you mean?" she asked.

"My name is Johnny Baxter. I'm not a new boy! I am Johnny Baxter," he said in frustration.

"How can you be Johnny?" she asked. "You don't have freckles."

"It's because I did what you told me to do."

"What was that?" Connie asked.

"You told me that Jesus cares about our feelings, so I prayed and asked Jesus to take my freckles away."

Just then, the school bell rang and it was time to go in. Everyone went to their lockers to hang up their jackets. Tommy walked with Johnny and said, "If God took your freckles away, He must be really powerful."

"He is," said Johnny, shutting his locker. As everyone entered the classroom, Johnny went right over to his regular seat and sat down. Adam, the boy behind him, said, "Hey you! What do you think you are doing, sitting at Johnny's desk?"

Johnny turned around with a stern look. "I *am* Johnny," he said.
"No, you're not."
"Yes, I am."
"You can't be. You don't have any freckles!" said Adam.

Soon other kids joined in, shouting, "You're not Johnny Baxter! You're not Johnny Baxter!"

"Yes I am! Yes I am!"

The shouting grew louder and louder.

Mrs. Williams, their third grade teacher, was out in the hallway talking to the principal when she heard the commotion. She hurried into the classroom, grabbed her ruler, and began tapping it on her desk. "Boys and girls!! Boys and girls!!" she shouted in a louder voice than normal. "Quiet down. Quiet down. What is this noise all about?" She looked around the room trying to figure out what was going on.

As soon as the children got quiet, Adam raised his hand.

"Yes?" asked Mrs. Williams.

Adam stood up and explained, "This boy is sitting in Johnny Baxter's seat. He says he is Johnny, but he sure doesn't look like him!"

Tommy piped up, "He isn't Johnny. He doesn't have any freckles!"

Miriam Snyder, the smartest girl in class, raised her hand.

"Do you have something to say, Miriam?" asked Mrs. Williams.

"Yes, thank you. I was wondering," she said, "if he isn't Johnny, then why did he go right over and sit in Johnny's seat?"

"Good point!" replied Mrs. Williams. "He does look a little bit like Johnny. I suppose there is only one way to find out. Let's have him come up here in front and tell us what is really going on.

Johnny would have normally been trembling at the thought of having to go up in front of the class to speak. But now that his freckles were gone, he felt more brave—not like the old Johnny at all. So, he got up and walked to the front of the room, up by the chalkboard.

"Go ahead," said Mrs. Williams. First, start by telling us your name."

"Why, Mrs. Williams? Don't you know who I am?" he asked in disbelief.

Johnny was beginning to feel like this was all a bad dream. "Ahem…," he began, as he cleared his throat. "My name is Johnny Baxter."

Some of the kids jeered. "Yea, right!!" or "You're not Johnny!" they shouted.

"Children, children, settle down!" said Mrs. Williams in a stern voice. She looked directly at Johnny and said, "If you are Johnny, then tell us what happened to your freckles."

Once again, Johnny began to tell his story. He told how some of the kids had called him names like "Freckle Head" day after day. "And then last Friday," he continued, "Connie Sims told me to pray to Jesus because Jesus cares about everything that concerns us. I figured, if Jesus would take my freckles away, maybe the kids would like me more and not be so mean to me, but I guess I was wrong."

Mrs. Williams noticed as Johnny spoke that many of the students hung their heads or had tears in their eyes. She said, "Jesus must really love you a lot to have taken away your freckles." Finally realizing that he was Johnny, she continued, "I believe He answered your prayer because He is God, and nothing is impossible for Him."

Mrs. Williams told Johnny to go back to his seat and gather his math book, paper and pencil. "I need to have you leave," she said, "so that that I may talk to your classmates. I'll write a note for you to give to Mrs. Lane down in the office, letting her know the reason you are coming down. When you get to the office, you may start working on page twenty-three in your math book. And, take your reader in case you get your math finished before I send Connie down to get you."

Johnny went to his desk to gather his things. As soon as the teacher handed him the note for Mrs. Lane, he walked out of the room and headed down the hallway.

Mrs. Williams walked over to her desk and sat down. "Boys and girls," she began, "this has been quite a morning. A miracle has happened. The Lord has taken Johnny's freckles away. I must say, though, I really liked Johnny better with freckles, and I know the Lord did, too. The Bible says," she continued, "that everything that the Lord made is good and is pleasing to Him. Johnny's freckles were pleasing to the Lord, but He loves Johnny so much that He answered his prayer. The Lord made all of us different and we are all special in His eyes. The Bible says we are fearfully and wonderfully made. Just because Johnny had freckles doesn't mean that he should be called names or made fun of. It just means that he was made to look unique."

She glanced around the room. "Some of the boys and girls in this classroom haven't been very kind to Johnny and have hurt his feelings so badly, he felt he had to get rid of his freckles in order to have friends. It is so sad to think he felt this way," she said. "The Lord is not pleased with the way some students have treated Johnny. I believe we need to ask Him for forgiveness. We need to ask Johnny for forgiveness too. Just as the Lord removed Johnny's freckles, He can also remove our sins," said Mrs. Williams.

Eddie raised his hand and Mrs. Williams called on him. He asked, "Is the Lord really that powerful?"

"Yes, He is."

"Does He really love us that much?"

"Yes, Eddie. He really does," said Mrs. Williams. She stood up and walked closer to the children's desks. "Boys and girls, would you like to make Jesus your Special Friend? Would you like to have Him in your heart so you can pray to Him when you need help?"

Some of the children said yes while others nodded their heads.

"I can help you do that," continued Mrs. Williams. "Everyone, bow your heads and close your eyes, so that we can pray.

Mrs. Williams prayed. She asked that the Lord would forgive each child of his or her sins. She thanked God for sending Jesus to die on the cross for their sins and asked Him to come into their hearts and be their Lord and Savior. She prayed that they would always live for Him.

23

"Boys and girls, keep Jesus in your heart and pray to Him when you need help. Later, we'll talk about the Bible and the help it will give you too," said Mrs. Williams. "Now before we have Johnny come back in the room, we should decide what we are going to do about what happened today and how we are going to treat Johnny. Does anyone have any ideas?"

Tommy was the first to speak up. "I won't call Johnny Freckle Head any more. And I won't be mean to him either."

Eddie added, "I think we should all be Johnny's friends from now on."

Then Connie shared, "I think we need to try harder to love each other."

"All of those are good ideas," replied Mrs. Williams. "Connie, you may go down and get Johnny now. While Connie is gone, I would like for all to get out your math books," said Mrs. Williams.

Connie walked out of the room and headed down the hallway to the office. When she got there, Johnny was reading. "Hi," said Connie. "It's time to go back."

"Oh, good," said Johnny, "I was getting bored! What did Mrs. Williams talk about?" he asked as they walked back to the room.

"A whole bunch of stuff about how the kids were mean to you."

"Hmmm..." Johnny muttered to himself in a thoughtful kind of way.

When they arrived at the classroom door, Mrs. Williams said, "Johnny, please stay up here by my desk. Your classmates have something to say to you. Would someone like to start?" she asked.

Tommy stood up. "I'm not going to call you Freckle Head any more," he said, sitting down quickly as if he was embarrassed.

Bojo stood up next and said, "I liked you better with freckles. I think we all should pray to the Lord and ask Him to give you your freckles back."

"Yeah!" resounded the students.

Eddie said, "Yeah, we liked the old Johnny better. You looked better with freckles. I will even pray for you."

Connie spoke up next. "Will you forgive us?"

"What do you think, Johnny?" asked Mrs. Williams.

Johnny stammered. "I forgive you," he said.

Everyone cheered.

"All right!" Mrs. Williams said. "Let's all pray to the Lord, Dear Lord Jesus, we thank You for answering Johnny's prayer and for taking his freckles away. We are now asking You, Lord, to do one more miracle and give Johnny back his freckles. In Jesus' name, we pray. Amen."

Later, when school let out that afternoon, Johnny walked over to Mr. Green's apple orchard to pray. He thanked Jesus for the kids being kind to him and asked Jesus to forgive him for thinking bad things about them. He also asked Jesus if He would give him back his freckles. Every day after school that week, Johnny stopped by Mr. Green's apple orchard and prayed. But his freckles didn't come back.

Friday morning, Johnny got up very early and left the house before anyone else. When he reached the apple orchard, he got down on his knees under the big apple tree. "Dear Jesus," he pleaded, "I don't know why You haven't answered my prayer, but if there is anything I have done to make You mad at me, please forgive me." He started to cry and said, "Please, Lord, answer my prayer."

Chapter 5
The Lord's Answer

"What is that noise?" asked Rosey Freckle. "It sounds like someone is crying."

"Why, look down there!" said Samuel Freckle, pointing down under the tree. "It's Johnny—he's back, and it looks like he's crying alright. I wish we could help him feel better."

"Listen, Freckles! I know how to help! I just heard from the Lord," exclaimed Pete Freckle, "and He says we are to get back on Johnny's face right away!"

"Thank goodness!" cried Harry Freckle. "I thought we were going to be stuck up here on these apples forever."

Naomi Freckle chimed in. "I was afraid Mr. Green would come and pick these apples and we would never get back on Johnny's face. I miss my home on the tip of his nose."

"Hey Pete, how on earth are we supposed to get way down there to Johnny's face?" asked Rosey Freckle.

But suddenly, before Pete could say a word, hundreds of angel freckles flew in from above and swooped down to pick up Johnny's freckles. The freckles hopped on the angels' backs and rode down to Johnny's face. Soon enough they were all back where they started on Johnny's forehead, nose, and cheeks.

Johnny had no idea that his freckles were back. He wiped away his tears, got up from under the tree, and slowly started toward school, thinking that the Lord still hadn't answered his prayer.

Tommy, Bojo, Eddie, and Connie were all standing together near the monkey bars when they saw Johnny walking into the schoolyard. As he got closer to them, Connie was the first to notice that Johnny's face was once again full of freckles.

"Your freckles are back! Your freckles are back!" she shouted. Eddie, Bojo, and Tommy all began to shout, "Hurray! Hurray!"

They all gathered around Johnny with big smiles on their faces saying, "Thank You, Jesus! Thank You, Jesus!" They cheered and jumped up and down with excitement, hugging each other and smiling from ear to ear. Johnny seemed to have the biggest smile of all, plus a little tear in his eye, as he looked up to heaven and whispered, "Thank You."

"Let's go in and tell Mrs. Williams!" said Connie as she led the boys inside.

After that day, no one ever called Johnny "Freckle Head" or "Freckle Face" again. And all the students at Greenville Christian School tried harder than ever to love one another.

About the Author

Sally Gomez has fulfilled a lifelong dream by writing *Too Many Freckles*. She has had the desire to write children's books for many years.

Sally has been passionately involved in a variety of children's ministries, teaching second grade girls in Missionettes at her former church, working at the day care there, and preparing Children's Chapel every other week.

She especially enjoys using puppets to teach boys and girls the Word of God. She is presently teaching once a month in Children's Church at Crosspointe Church, in Brooklyn, Michigan.

Besides writing, she loves to make handmade gifts for friends and family for Christmas, weddings, and even baby showers. Sally enjoys painting, illustrating, crocheting, and sewing.

She and her loving husband are retired and presently living in Brooklyn, Michigan along with their two adorable cats, Baby and Tula.

Sally has just finished two new books and is presently working on a third book as well as a sequel to *Too Many Freckles*.

To order additional copies of *Too Many Freckles* or to find out about other books by Sally Gomez or Zoë Life Publishing, please visit our website www.zoelifepub.com.

Zoë Life Publishing
P.O. Box 871066
Canton, MI 48187
(877) 841-3400
outreach@zoelifepub.com

Other books available by Zoë Life Publishing:

The Hidden Treasures of My Kingdom Pals:
Treasure of Trust
Written by Julie Page and Sabrina Adams
Illustrated by Mike Motz

Cassie and Mr. Ant
Written by Glenda Powell
Illustrated by Hazel Mitchell

Luke's 1st Haircut
Written by Catherine Marek
Illustrated by Hazel Mitchell

Sara's 1st Haircut
Written by Catherine Marek
Illustrated by Hazel Mitchell